This Book Belongs To

_____

First edition copyright ©2007 Fletcher Dale

All rights reserved. No part of this publication may be reproduced, stored in a retrieval system or transmitted in any form or by any means, electronic, mechanical, photocopying, recording or otherwise, without the prior written permission of the publisher.

National Library of Australia cataloguing-in-publication data: Dale, Fletcher

Hydro Flux Drops In, An Introduction to Anatomy

1st ed. Children's Picture Book

ISBN :978-0-9804220-2-3

Published by Fletcher Dale

Email: fletcherdale@protonmail.com
www.fletcherdaleart.com
Design and layout by Fletcher Dale

Other books by this author
Hydro Flux - A Story of Water
Hydro Flux - A Kids Guide to a Healthy Earth
Hydro Flux Feasts - A Kids Guide to a Healthy Diet
Special Agent H20 Hydro Flux Saves Laverockbay
Let's Move with Hydro Flux - A Kids Guide to a Healthy Body

Special Agent H₂O
Hydro Flux Drops In

Fletcher Dale

I'm Special Agent H20,
Hydro Flux in the flow,
Yesterday I was in the rain,
Today I rushed on down a drain.

Then into a pipe wide and long,
With other drops I ran along,
Until someone turned on a tap,
Someone in a bright red cap.

Under the cap, a boy named Fred,
Needs a drink to cool his head,
Down I go with a gulp and grin,
In Fred's tummy I now swim.

While I'm here I'll take a look,
Explore Fred's body in this book,
So many parts with a story to tell,
Let's see how a body works so well.

I'm in Fred's stomach with his lunch,
There'is lots of noise, munch and crunch,
The size of a sausage, stretched to full,
Mixing and churning, push and pull,
Gastric juice has begun an attack,
Breaking food down inside this sack.

When all the food is broken down,
It turns to soup and slops around,
Juice is squirting everywhere,
Changing food, I better take care,
Vitamins and minerals soak right in,
Passing through your stomach's skin.

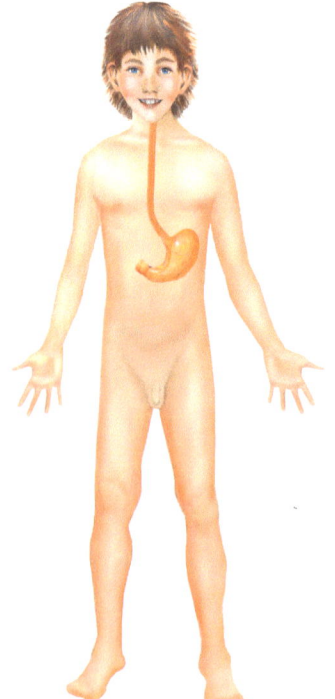

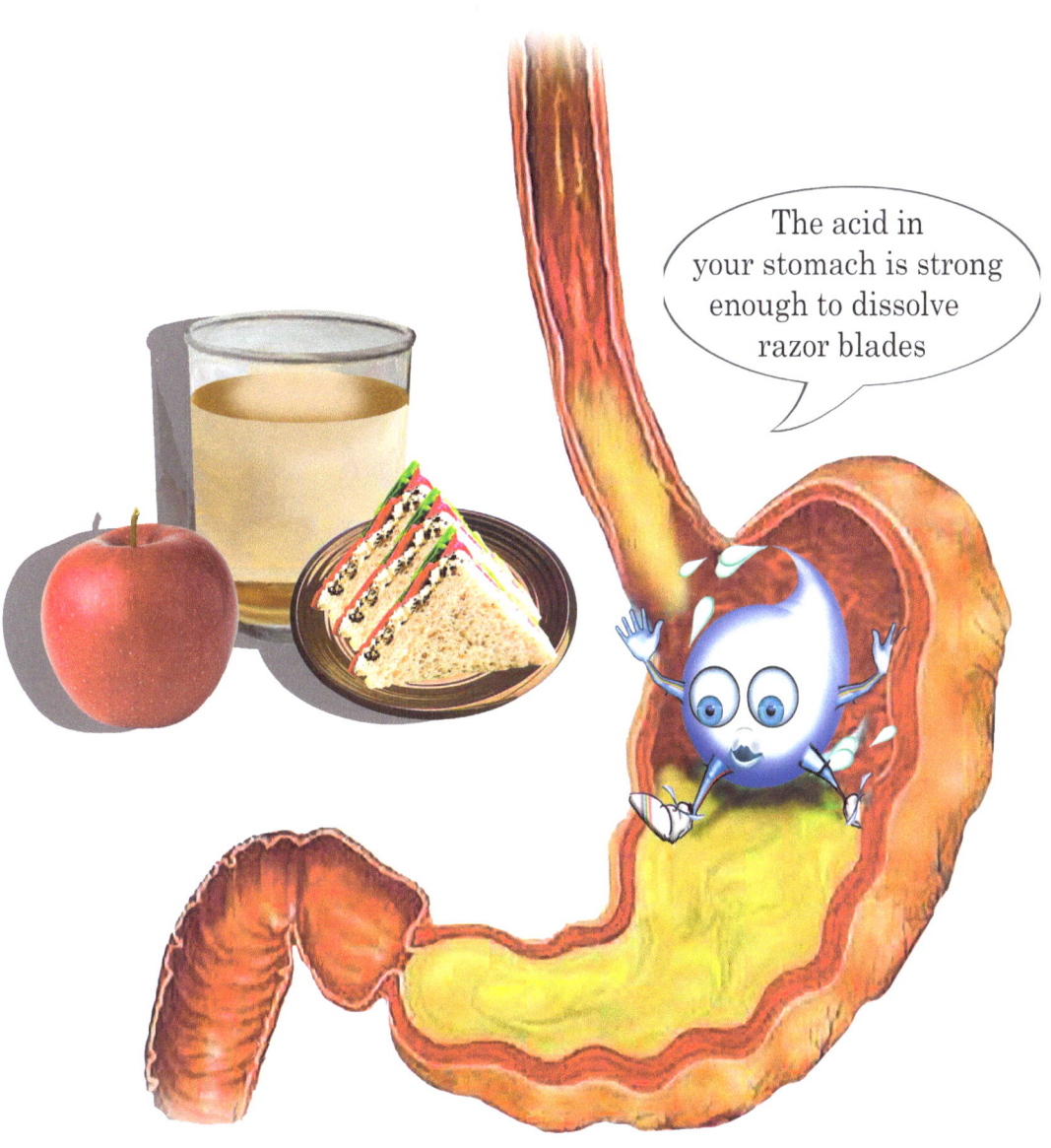

Stomach

Whoops! I just went in a squirt,
Into a tube, better stay alert,
This tube is like a curled up snake,
A process plant for goodness sake.

The intestines work to separate,
Digesting, absorbing all Fred ate,
Muscles push the food along,
Fred's body never gets it wrong,
The nutrients pass into the blood,
What's left behind looks like mud.

Now all the good bits have disappeared,
Leaving only waste and rubbish here,
This keeps on moving down and out,
That's what the toilet's all about.

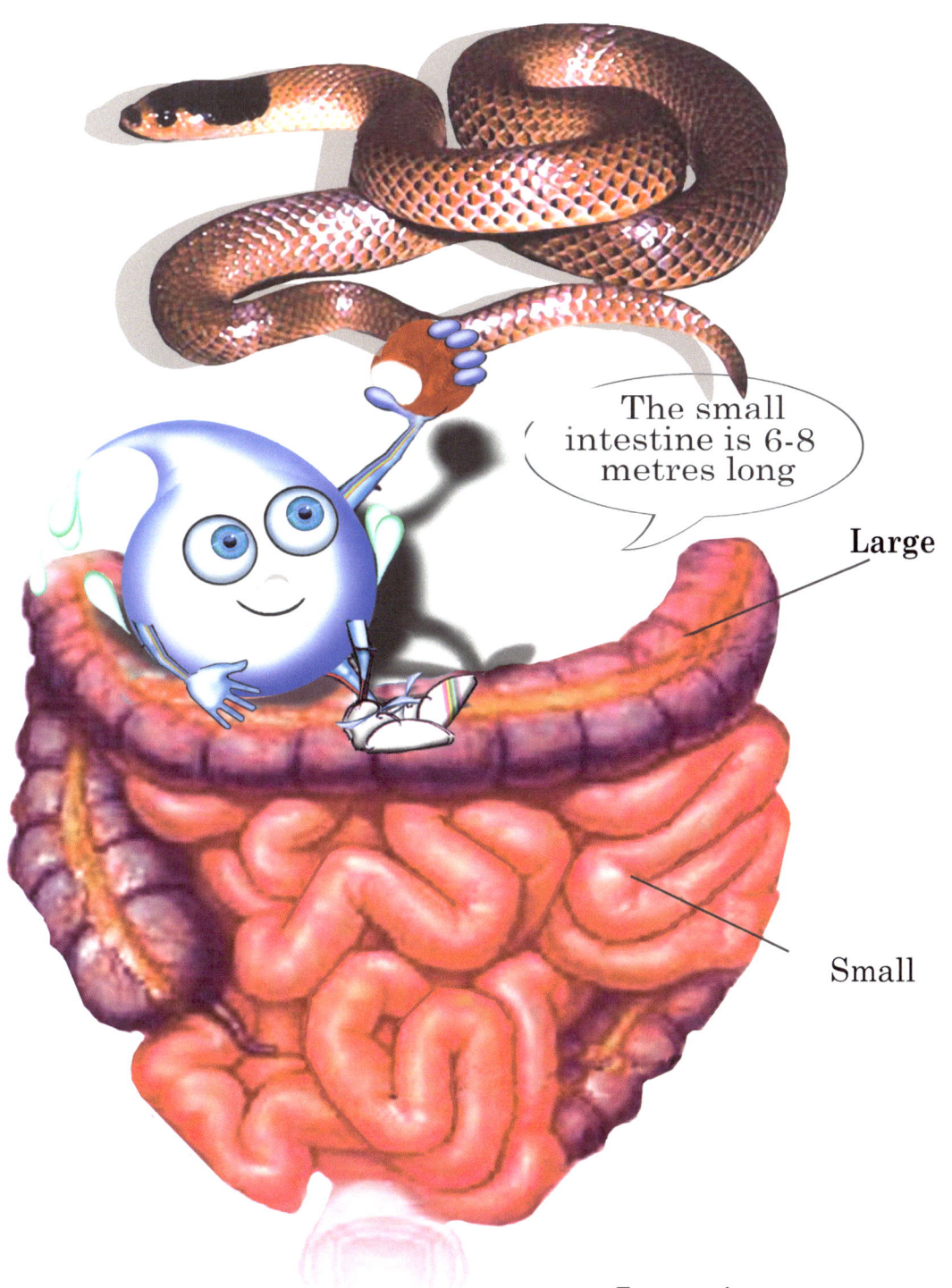

Intestines

Good bits from the food have gone,
Into Fred's blood stream quickly drawn,
Inside here flows a mighty river,
His flowing blood makes me shiver.

Blood moves about from head to toes,
Delivering food everywhere it goes,
Vtamins and minerals reach every cell,
This healthy blood feeds Fred well.

Arteries go away from the heart,
Carrying oxygen to every body part,
Blood is also like a garbage truck,
Collecting rubbish and all the muck,
Veins carry blood back to the heart,
Let's take a ride and find this part.
part.

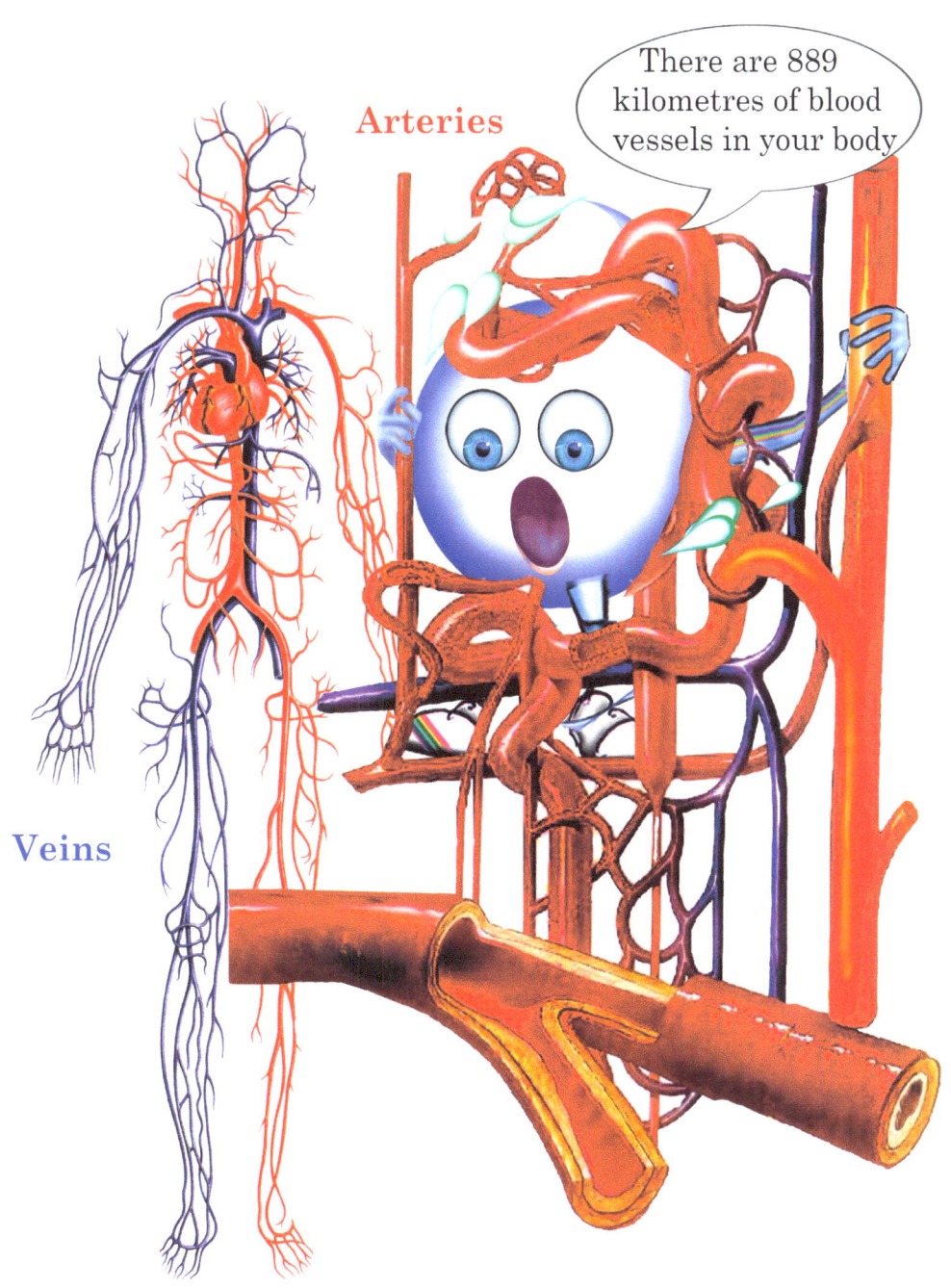

Blood Vessels

Here in the middle of Fred's chest,
His amazing heart never takes a rest,
No other muscle is this strong,
Hard at work his whole life long.

I listen to that thump, thump, thump,
As Freddy's heart goes pump, pump, pump,
It works away with a squeeze and push,
I hear the blood whoosh, whoosh, whoosh!

Its job is to pump the blood around,
When Fred runs it starts to pound,
Beating over 100,000 times a day,
It's pushing me hard on my way.

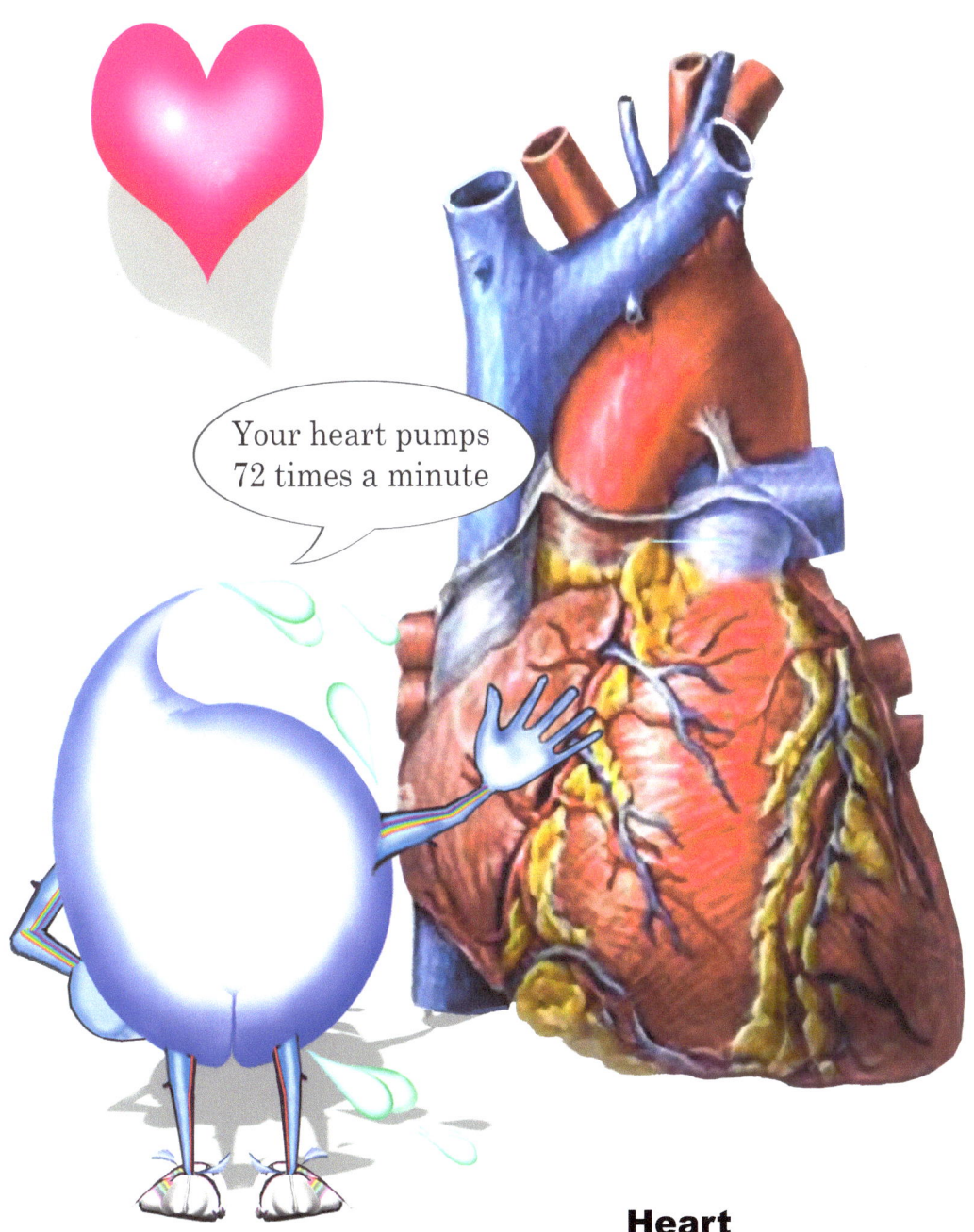

So now I move along the river,
To pay a visit to Fred's liver,
The largest organ of them all,
We need to pay this one a call.

Here sits a chemical factory,
What it does is quite a story,
It changes waste from the food,
Cleans the body of things no good.

Like a sponge it just soaks things up,
Works at separating all the muck,
If Fred has too many lollies to eat,
It changes sugar and stores it neat.

As Fred's body works each day,
It produces waste,
That won't go away,
But the liver it just soaks it in,
Working like a garbage bin.

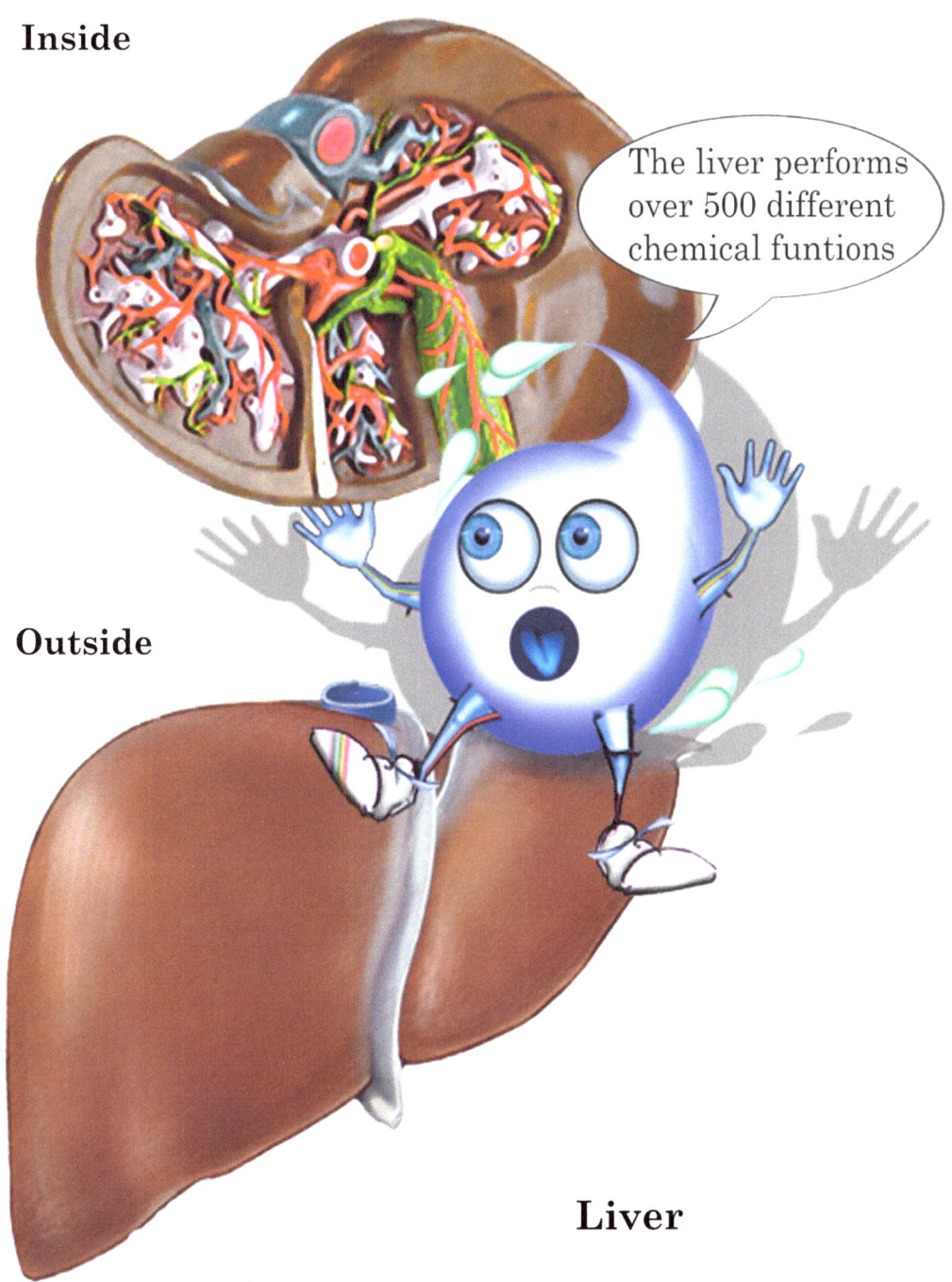

If Fred cuts his toe and it bleeds,
His liver makes just what he needs,
To make his blood lump and clot,
Makes sure he won't lose the lot.

Platelets floating in the blood,
Help plug the leak to stop a flood,
Sensing oxygen in the air,
They go to work to trap and snare.

They then break up to form a net,
Catching red blood cells which get,
To quickly form a hardened scab,
You can see all this in a science lab.

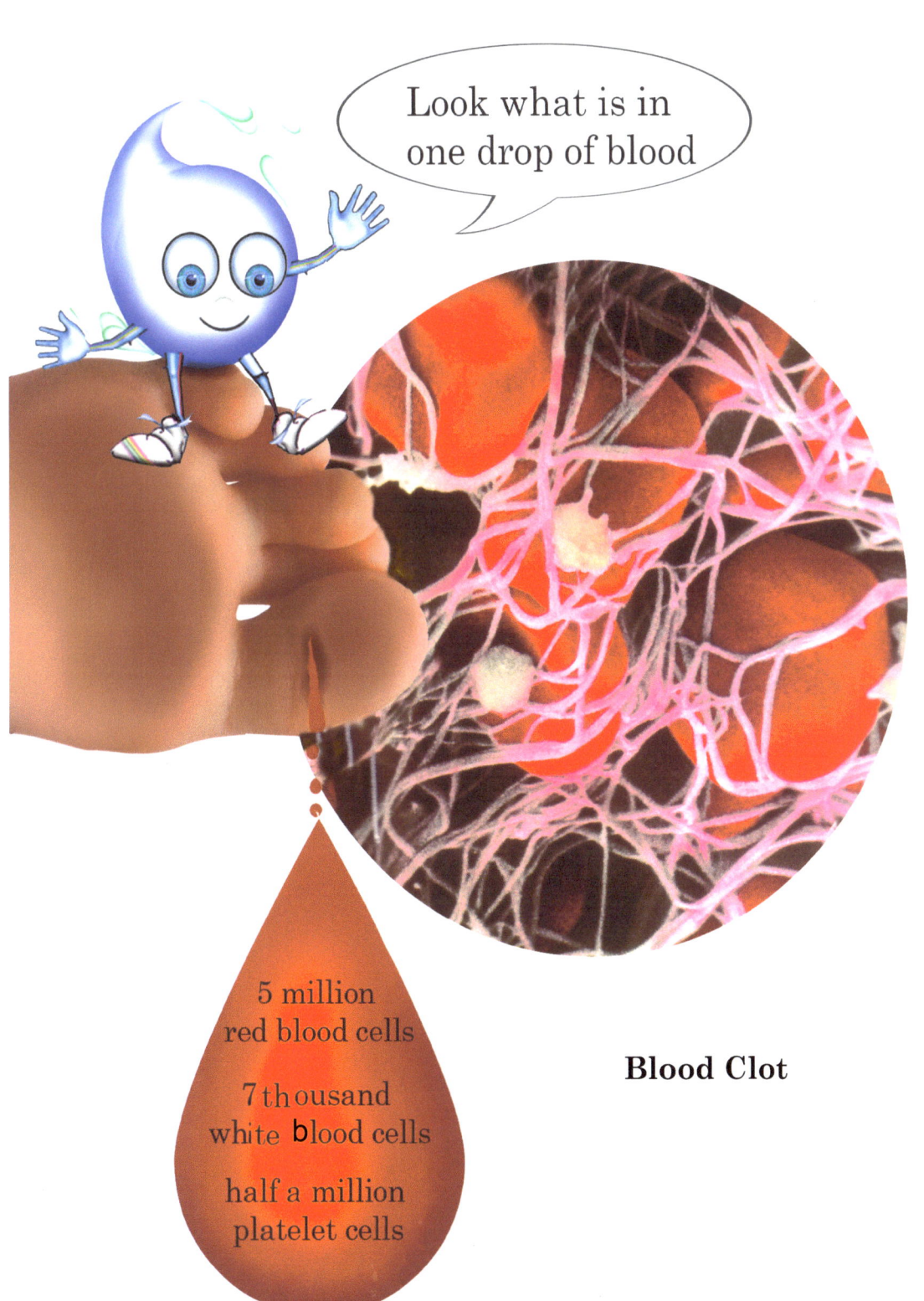

Blood Clot

Back to the river the rubbish flows,
Off to the kidneys is where it goes,
Not real big, shaped like a bean,
In goes the blood to filter and clean.

With an urgent and a constant need,
To clean the system with great speed,
Kidneys handle the water works,
Checking levels and where it lurks,

At work to keep the water balance,
A vital part of Fred's defence,
Extra water and all the waste,
Is sent to the bladder in great haste.

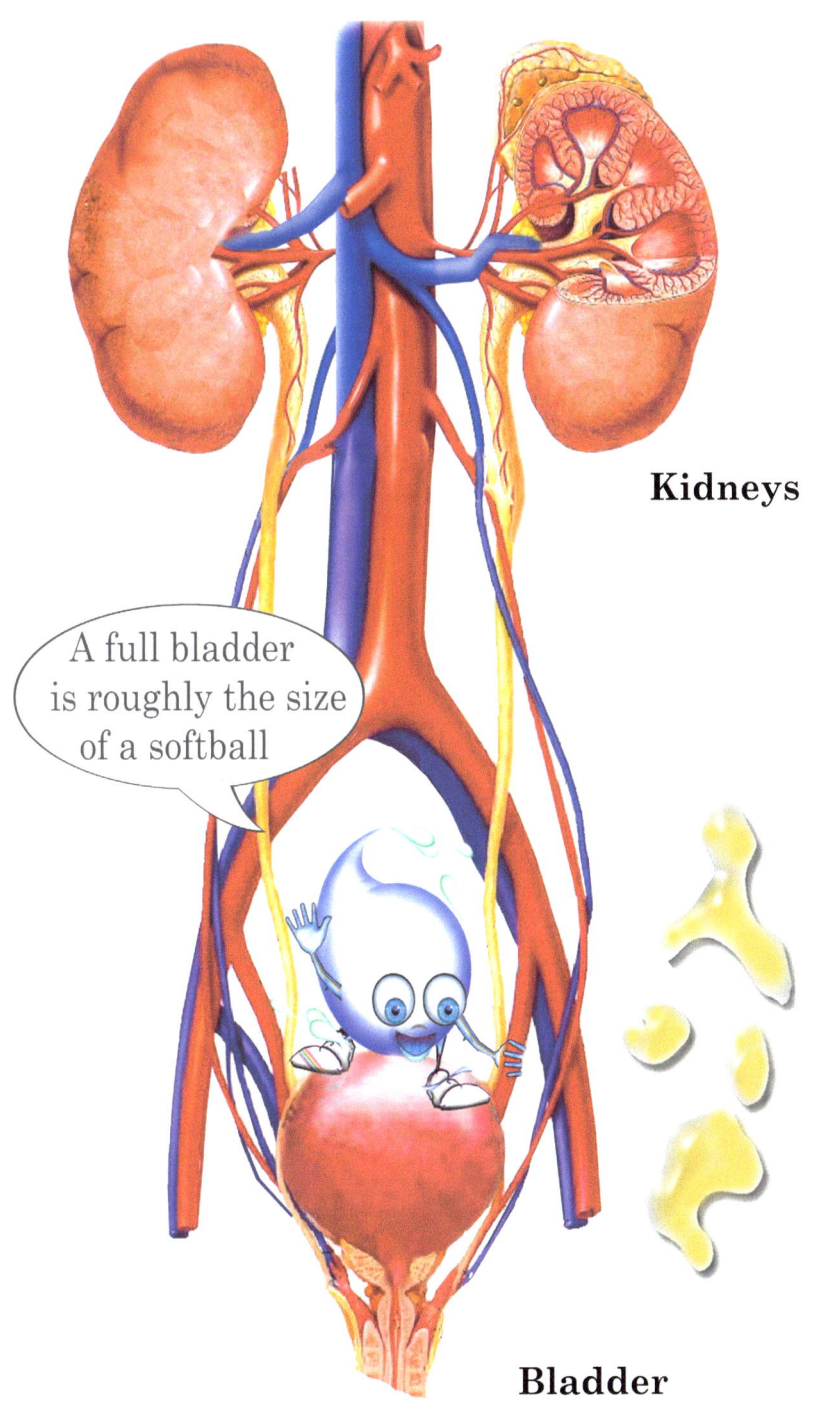

All day urine trickles out of each kidney,
Full of waste and water, it makes a journey,
To the bladder, which stretches like a balloon,
Sends a message to the brain, better do wee soon.

I might just make a getaway,
Or Fred will pass me out that way.
I'd rather stay inside his blood,
Keep on moving with the flood!

Fred is running in a rush,
Air flies in with a mighty gush,
With a puff and a whoosh,
And a whoosh and a puff,
The ride in here is pretty rough.

When Fred runs,
He needs more air,
Without it he will go nowhere,
But dirty air makes lungs whine,
Gives them just the hardest time.

Let's go on exploring more,
Hope you remember all we saw,
So many parts all strung together,
Your body is a special treasure.

Now I'm down inside Fred's lung,
Very strange the way it's hung,
Looks like a tree upside down,
Boy you ought to hear the sound.

Of the air that Freddy breathes,
The good stuff stays,
The bad stuff leaves,
On oxygen his body feeds,
And plenty of it for his needs.

In the top most branches of the tree,
So very tiny you couldn't see,
Red blood cells move to do a swap,
Rather like a transfer shop.

They collect oxygen, turn bright red,
This will keep Fred's muscles fed,
Carbon dioxide, the muscles waste,
Is left behind, breathed out in haste.
White blood cells help fight disease,
Seizing all the germs with ease.

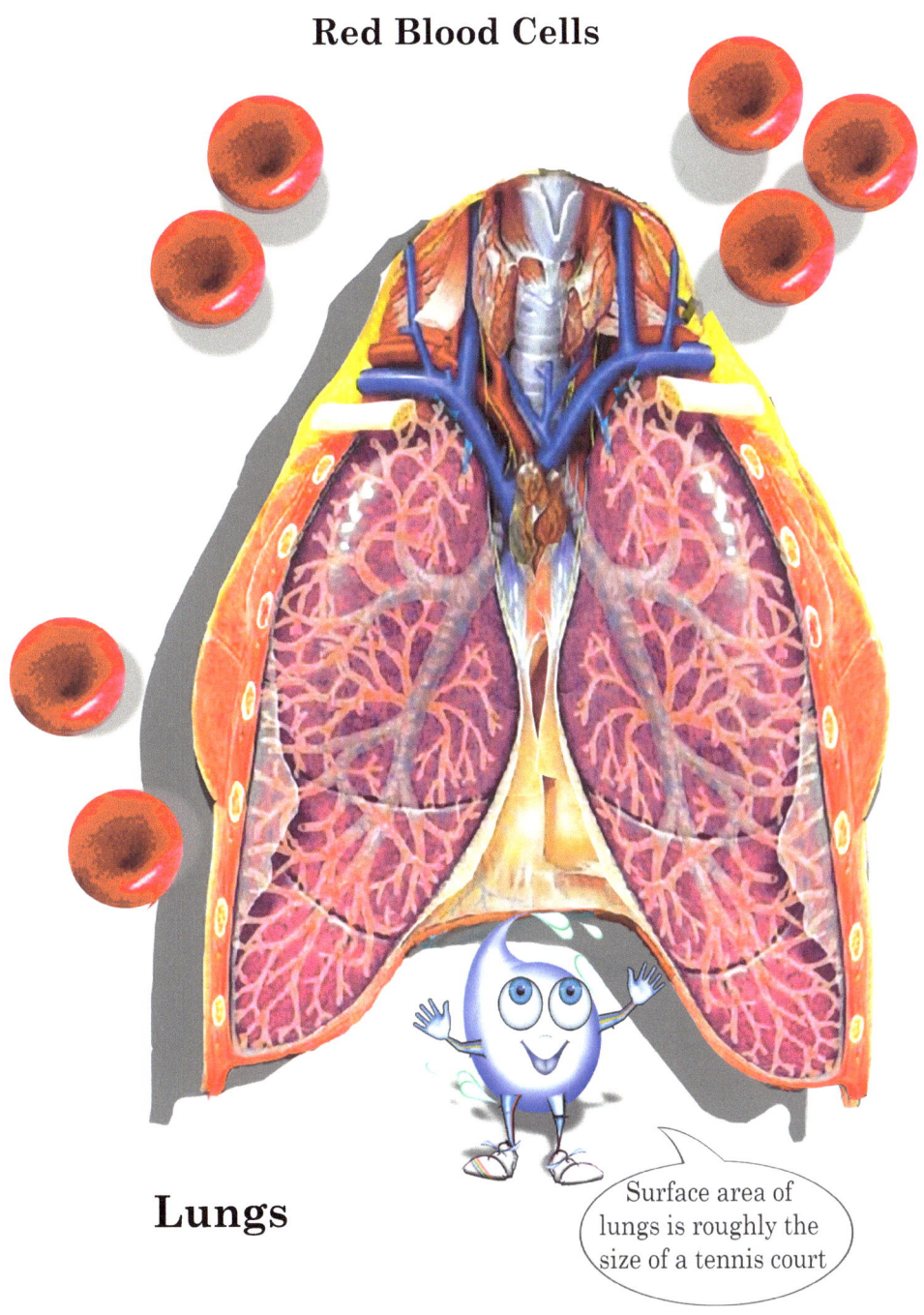

A tiny cell is so very small,
It's hard to tell it is there at all,
A microscope would let you see,
Teeny weeny dots of activity.

I really had a great surprise,
A body so smart, a body is wise.
Cells function in rythm and harmony,
Millions and millions, tinier than me,
Floating inside an inland sea
Millions of drops exactly like me.

With skin that lets stuff in and out, Cells stretch and grow and move about, They eat and breath and give off waste, Keep company and communicate. Some work to build, some to clean, A cell is one small mean machine.

Blood, bone, nerve and skin cells,
Liver, lung, kidney, hair cells.
Busy ants, not asking why,
Until cells get damaged, wear out and die,
But tricky things, they split apart,
To become a brand new cell with a fresh start.

Cells

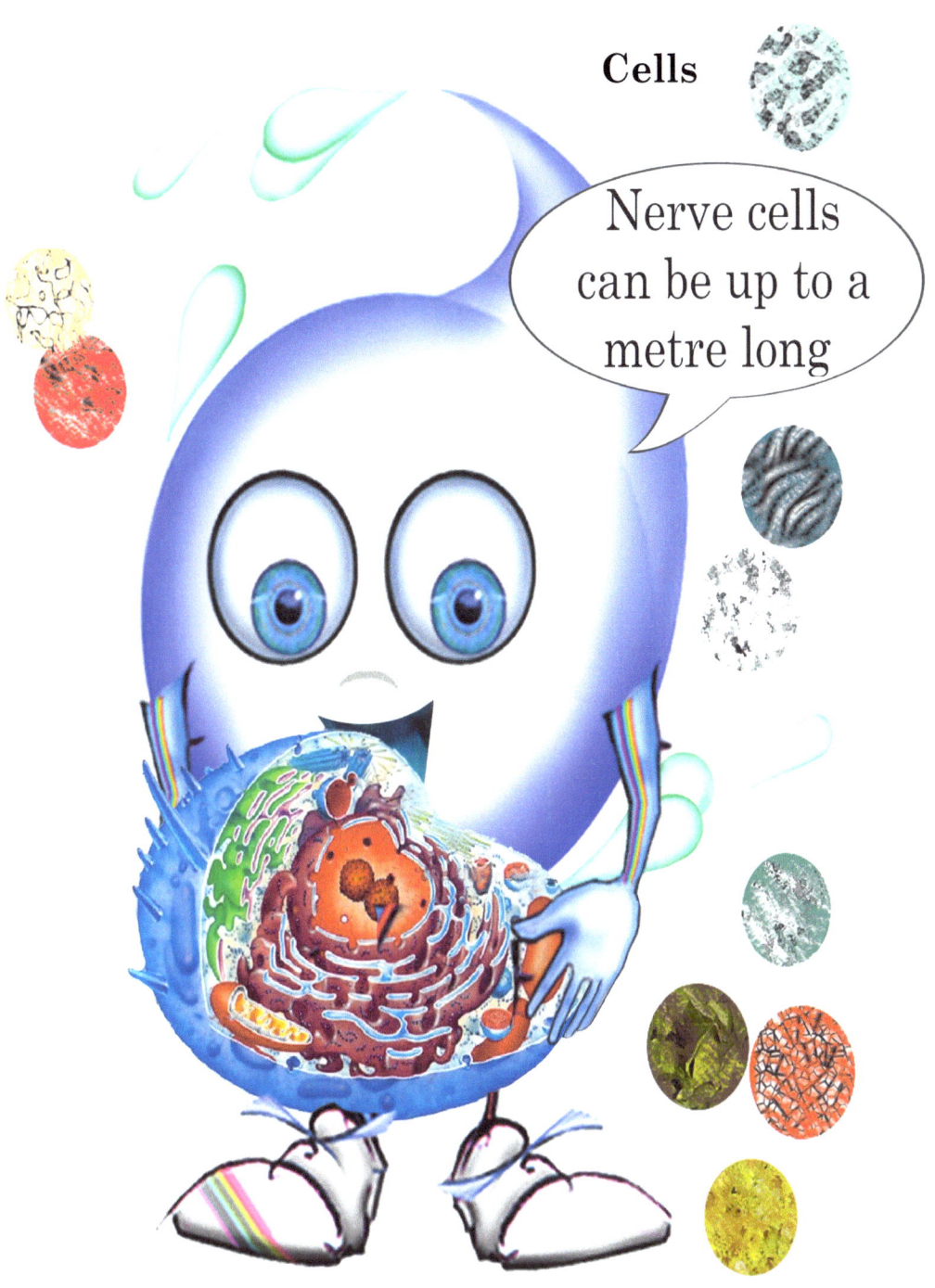

Nerve cells can be up to a metre long

Let's move along and look at bone,
A broken one would make Fred groan,
Without his bones he'd be like jelly,
Crawling around on his belly.

Without bones he'd be a blob of meat,
He couldn't walk or talk or eat,
A hollow space inside that's narrow,
Makes new blood in stuff called marrow.

Bones are different in shape and size,
206 in all, the biggest are in the thighs.
Most are very hard and strong,
So Fred can carry himself along.
Now let's get back in the river and flow,
See where next the flow will go.

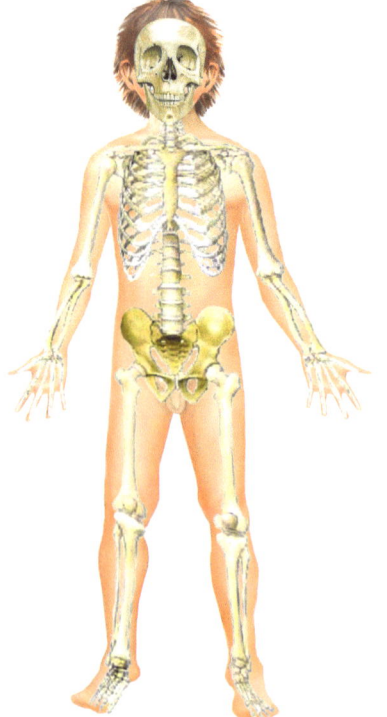

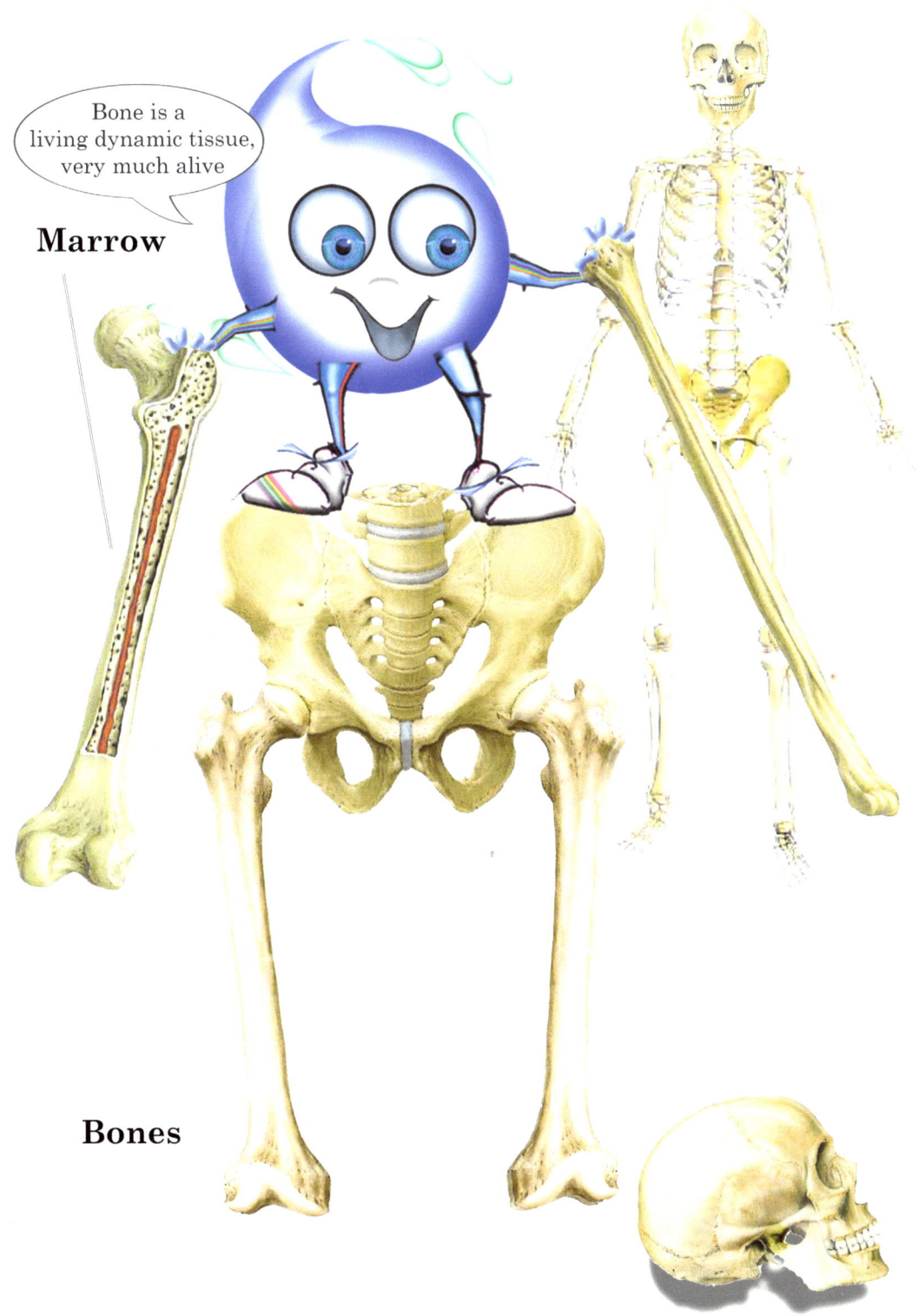

Muscles help Fred do everything,
Like pump his blood and let him grin.
Some muscles he can take control,
His legs will move when they're told.
Fred's heart, intestines and a blink,
Do their jobs when he doesn't think.

With over 600 muscles in his body,
Without them Fred just would not be.
All elastic tissue like rubber bands,
Lying close together in stripey strands,
Muscles work with bones to give,
Lots of power and strength to live.

Muscles attach to bones by tendons,
Withstanding tension during action,
These cords of tissue are very tough,
Attached so well, if Fred gets rough,
They just keep on, holding on,
To make Fred's body extra strong.

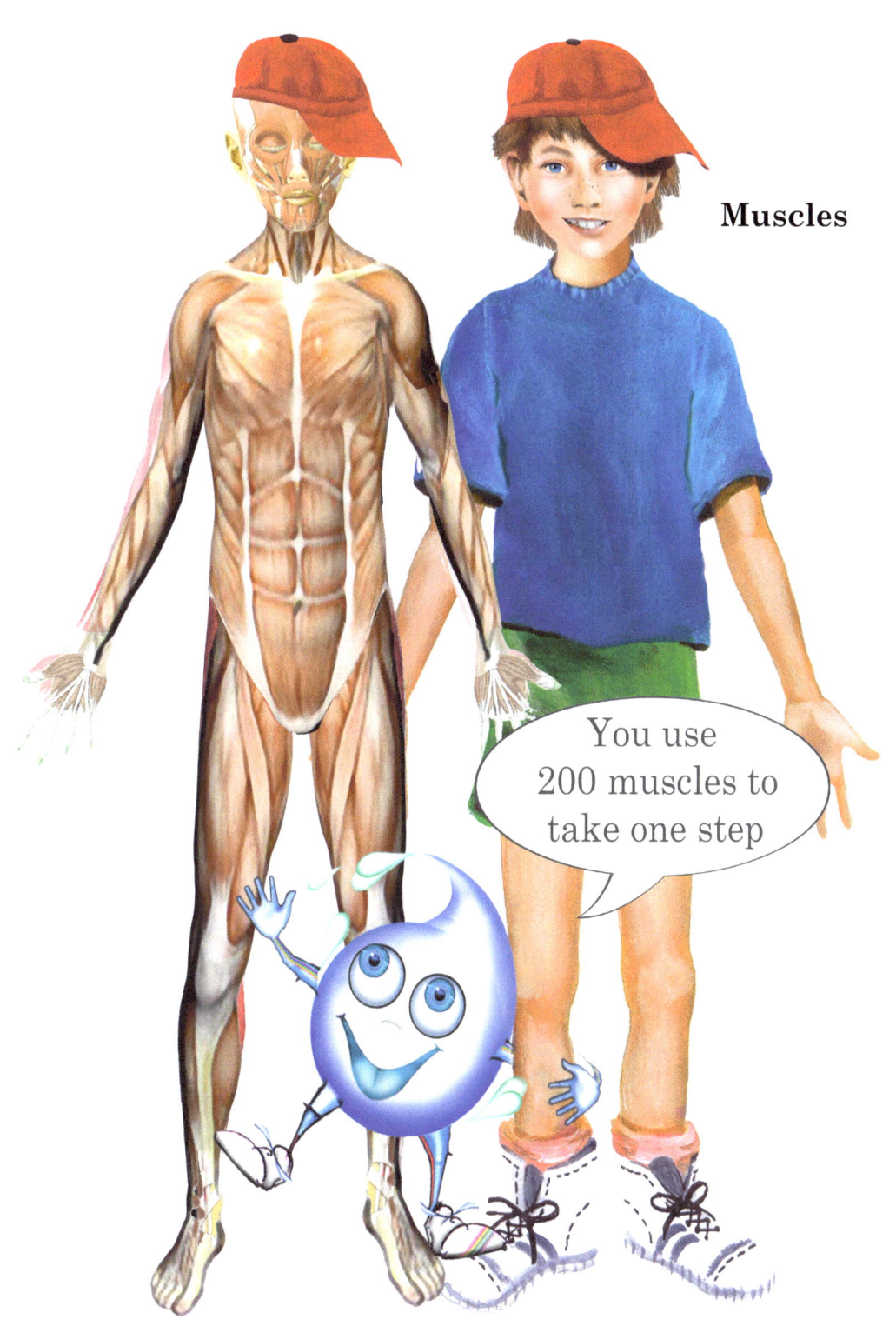

Muscles

You use 200 muscles to take one step

Now I find I'm in Fred's skin,
Like wrapping paper it holds him in.
Skin works to save Fred's body heat,
It also makes him look more neat.
Millions of sweat glands, his body's tool,
Air-condition to keep him cool.

The largest organ if you please,
It's the first defense against disease.
Protects from germs that hang about.
Keeps water in and water out.

When Fred feels heat, cold or pain,
His skin sends messages to his brain.
When he's cold he gets goose bumps,
They're really tiny warm up lumps.

It's color comes to you and me,
From something called heredity.
Red and yellow, black or white,
Skin is great, dark or light.

Let's float the river up Fred's back,
Climb his spine on bones which stack,
A strong and bendy rod that moves,
To twist and turn, each way it grooves.

Small bones which turn every way,
Let Fred's body bend and sway.
Ribs attach with tendons to Fred's spine,
Which supports his head, keeps him in line.

Spinal fluid runs inside to his brain,
Sending emails along a traffic lane,
From muscles, bones, blood and heart.
It carries information from every part.

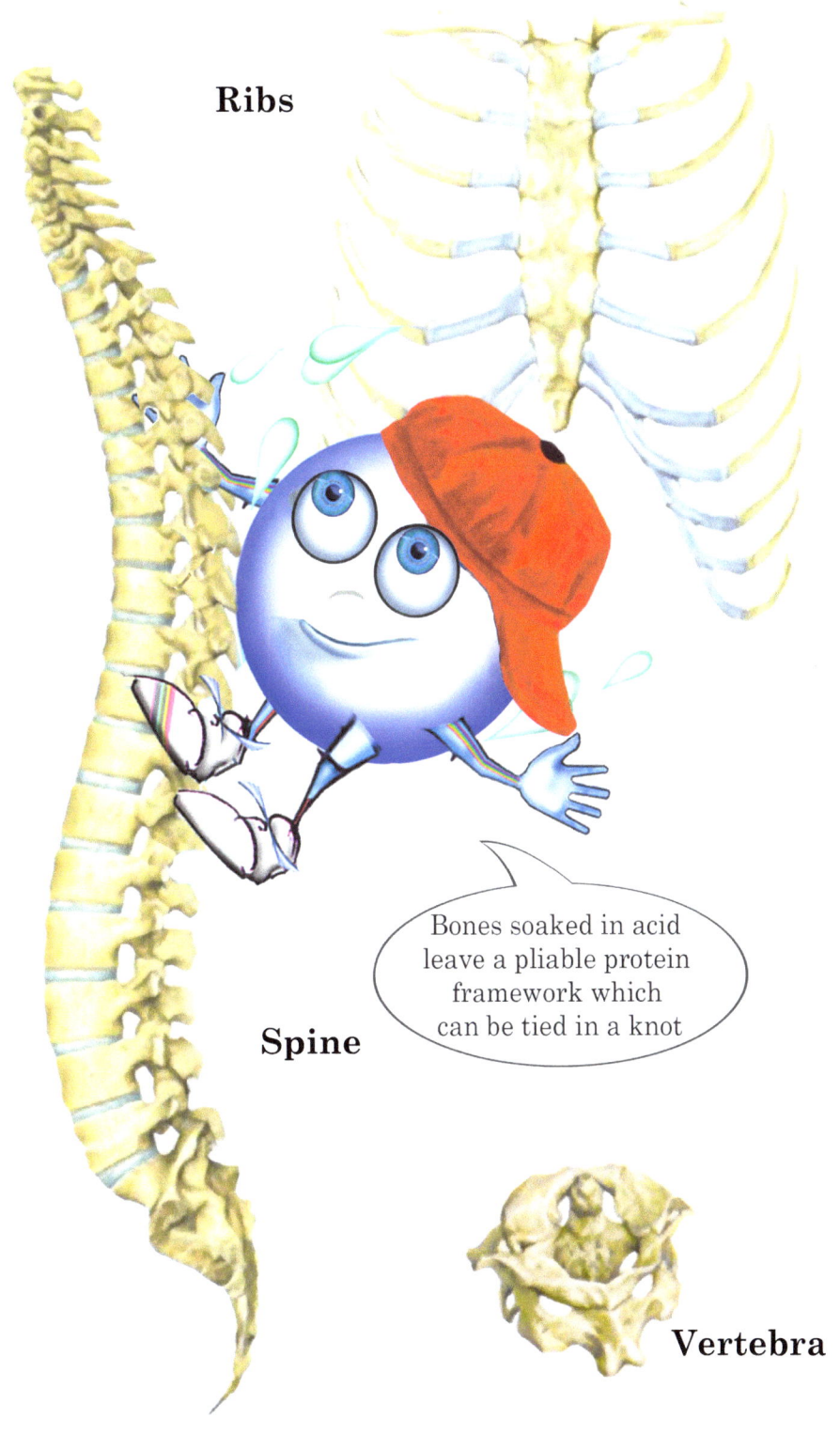

Ribs

Spine

Bones soaked in acid leave a pliable protein framework which can be tied in a knot

Vertebra

Fred's nervous system runs endless news,
Lets his brain know the body's views,
Twing ping ding, twing ping ding,
Like a busy phone nerves buzz and ring,
Transmitting messages day and night,
The nerves are never ever quiet.

Electric charges leap to and fro,
It's nerves that make your body go,
These tiny depots never touch,
But still they do so very much,
Just like you use electricity,
A body is busier than a big city.

Nerves

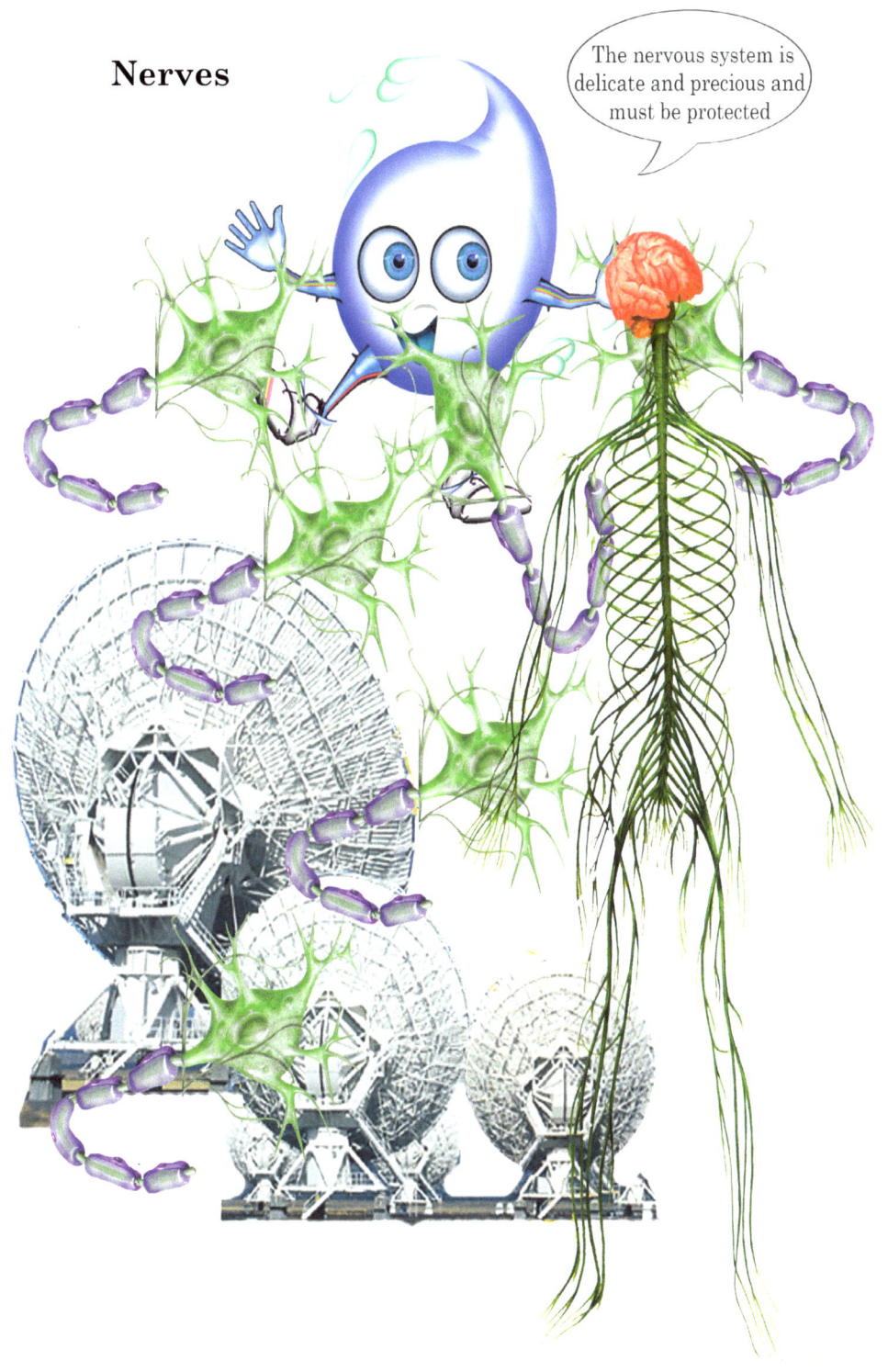

Fred's skull is very tough and strong,
Protects his brain from a knock or dong,
His brain looks like a big mushroom,
Here inside this special room.

Here in the centre of Fred's head,
A relay station knows all that's said,
It's here that every message goes,
From organs, limbs, hands and toes.
His brain is really a bundle of nerves,
Fred's whole body it quietly serves.

Buzz, ring, clink, buzz, ring, clink,
A busy brain goes think, think, think,
Information flies about,
Bringing in and sending out.

Fred dreams, feels and tastes from here,
When he's hungry or full of fear,
His reason, memory and his speech,
Back and forth the messages reach.

Everything Fred's body knows,
The brain is saying how it goes,
The greatest magic in the world,
Lies in his head all snug and curled.

Inside Fred's head I flow along,
Past his voice box, sing a song,
In his mouth I found this thing,
Without a tongue, he can't talk or sing.

His taste buds are like little bumps,
His teeth for chewing all the lumps,
His tongue will also help him swallow,
Feed the growl if his tummy's hollow.

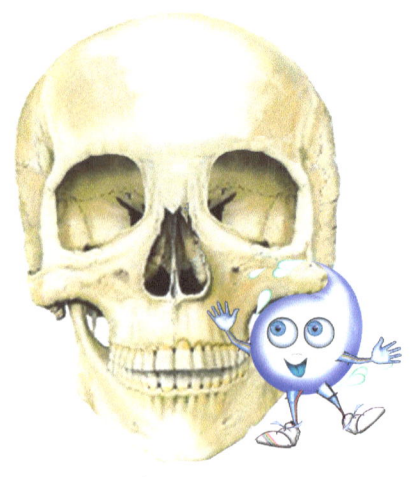

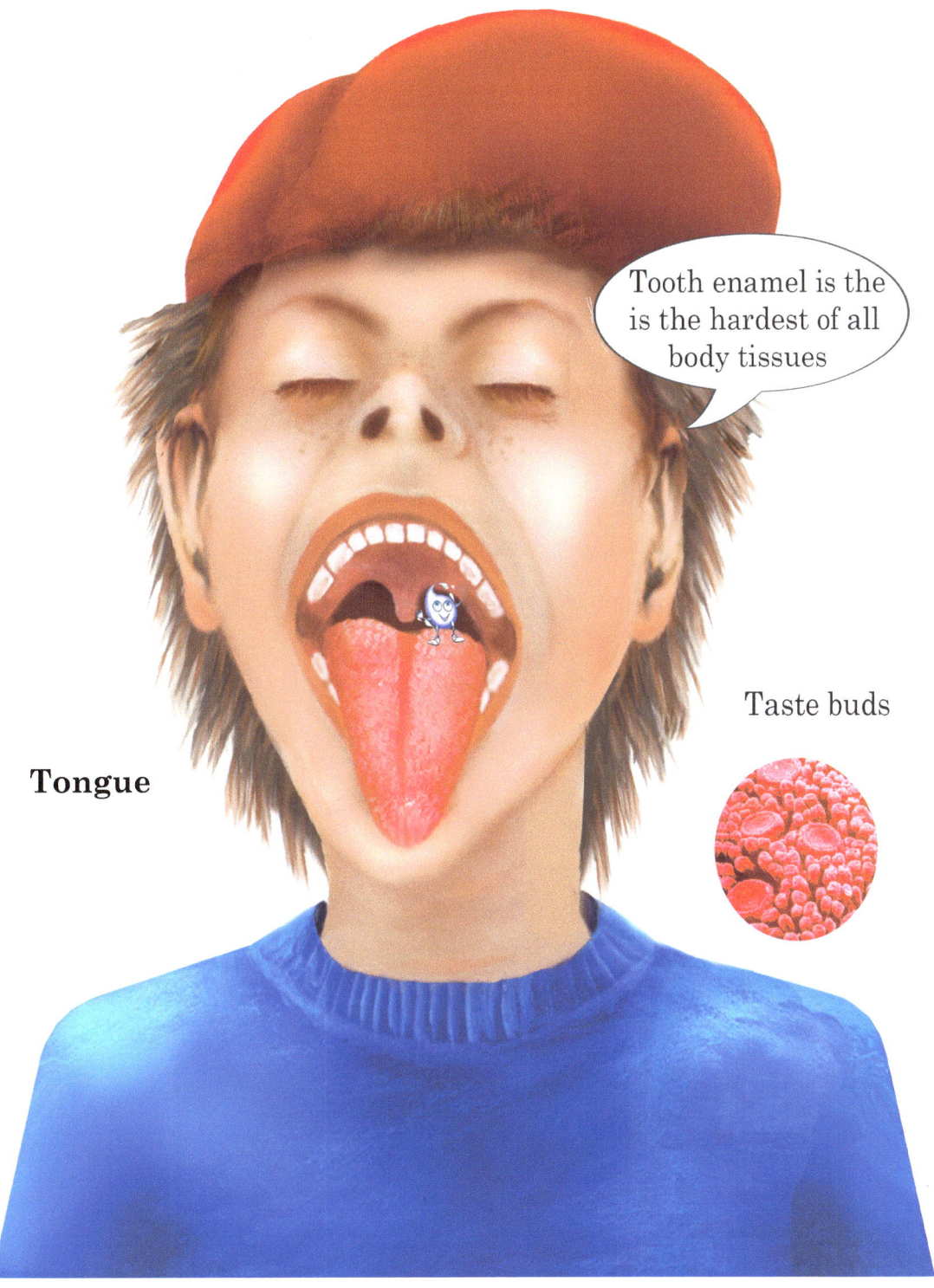

Tooth enamel is the is the hardest of all body tissues

Taste buds

Tongue

Let's take a look inside Fred's nose,
He'll use his nose to smell a rose,
His taste and smell work together,
Relying heaps upon each other.
As Fred breathes in, it cleans the air,
Sneezing clears the dirt trapped there.

Smells enter the nostrils then dissolve,
To stimulate nerves, yet they can't resolve,
What is that smell? Fred's mind will ask,
Nerves fire the brain to solve that task.

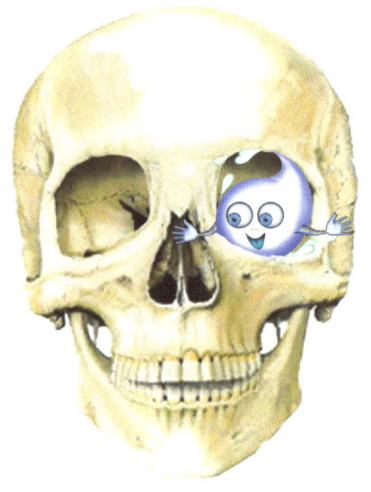

Nose

Smell sense cells

Odours help us remember events, feelings, and emotions which otherwise would be forgotten

Here we are inside Fred's ear,
That funny flap that let's him hear,
It's sticking out to catch the sound,
So Fred can hear what's all around.

Inside there lives a tiny drum,
A noisy sound or a little hum,
Will send it's message deep inside,
Where tiny hairs that vibrate hide.

These hairs will pass the message on,
Every word or noise or song,
Goes dancing fast inside Fred's head,
To the whiz computer to be read.

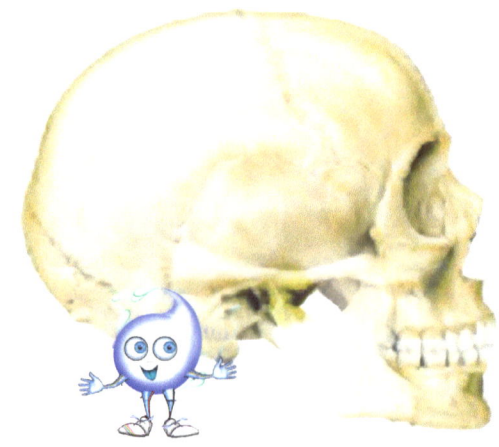

Ear Drum

Fluid which swirls when the head moves helps us maintain posture and balance

Now with a hop, skip and jump,
There is a bony brow which makes a lump,
Protecting eyes blue and bright,
Wonderous things giving sight.

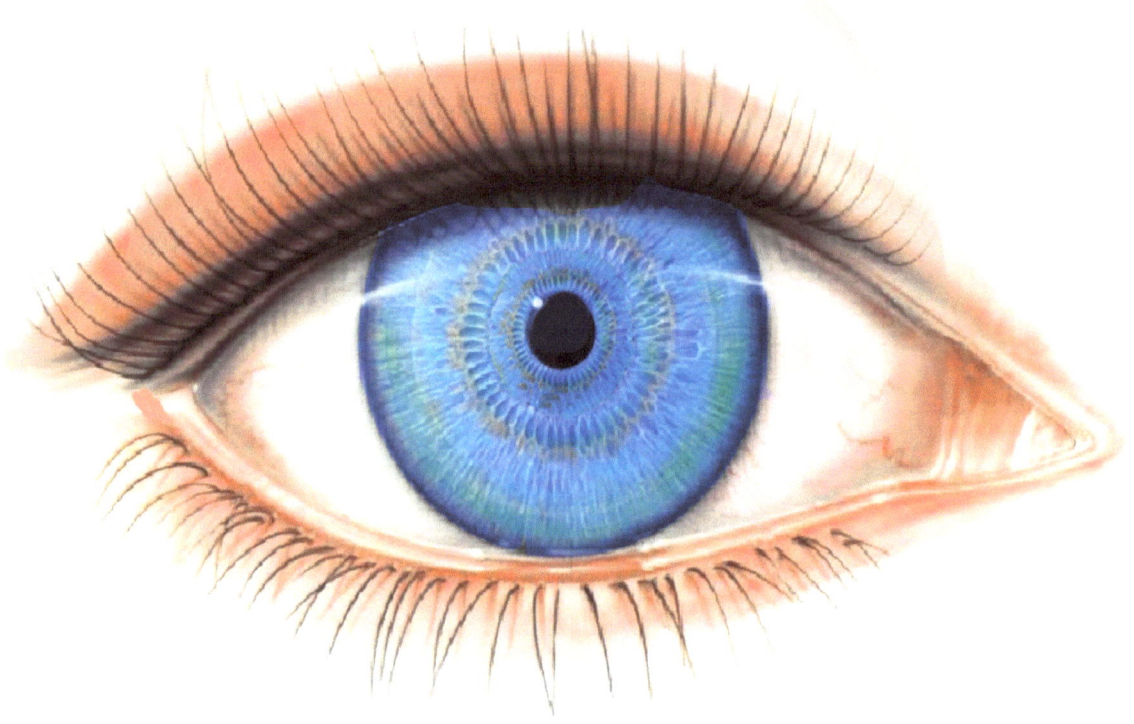

Like a jelly filled ping pong ball,
Most is hiding but not all,
A miniture camera plays with light,
Works at day time and at night.

Eyes are cleaned when Freddy blinks,
His pupil grows and it shrinks,
In sunlight it will almost hide,
At night time it is open wide.

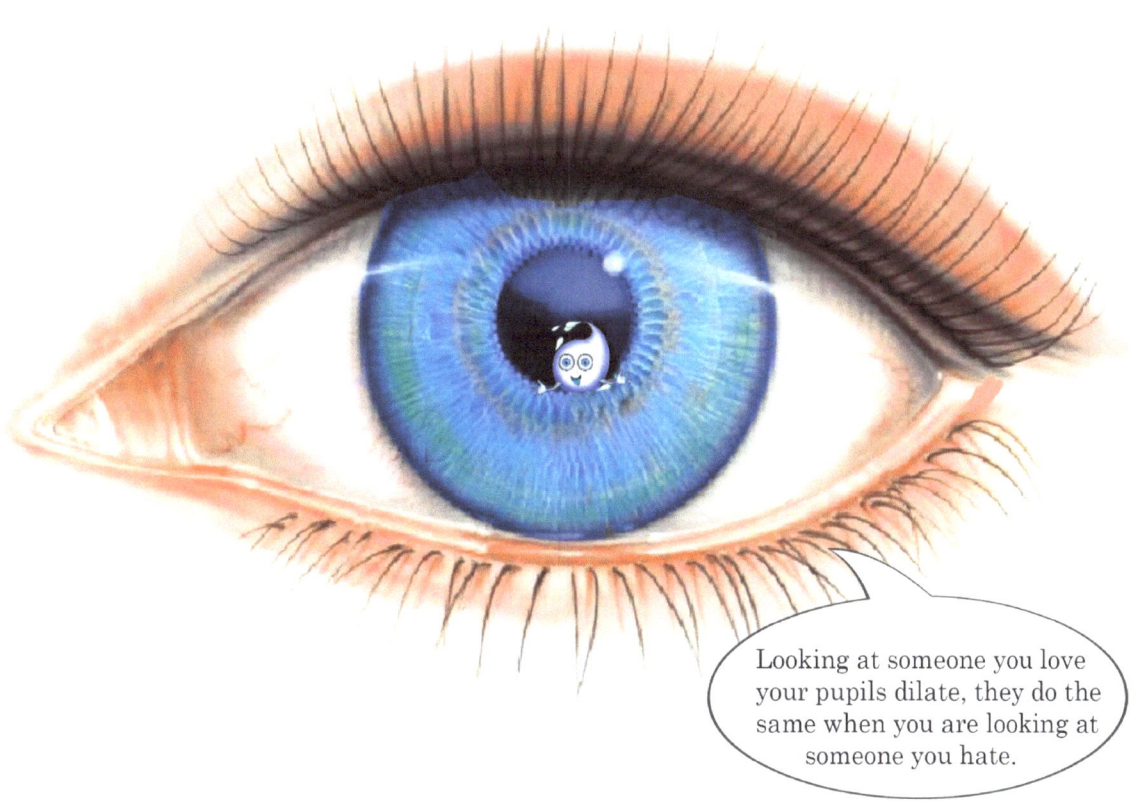

Looking at someone you love your pupils dilate, they do the same when you are looking at someone you hate.

Most everything that Fred will learn,
Comes through eyes that blink and turn,
They wash themselves by making tears,
Cry from sadness, joy or fears.

Wow, how about that!
I just slipped out,
What's Freddy got to cry about,
His body's great, so diverse,
Fred is a minature universe.

Seen from inside, it's incredible,
Beautiful, complex, unbelievable.
Serving Fred with intelligence,
In awesome, subtle silence.

Now you know what'is inside,
Live in your skin, take pride,
Know your body, be aware.
Love your body, take care.

Drink lots of water, H_2O,
It makes the blood and fluid flow,
Get wise how water works for you!
And become a Special Agent too!

Go H_2O!

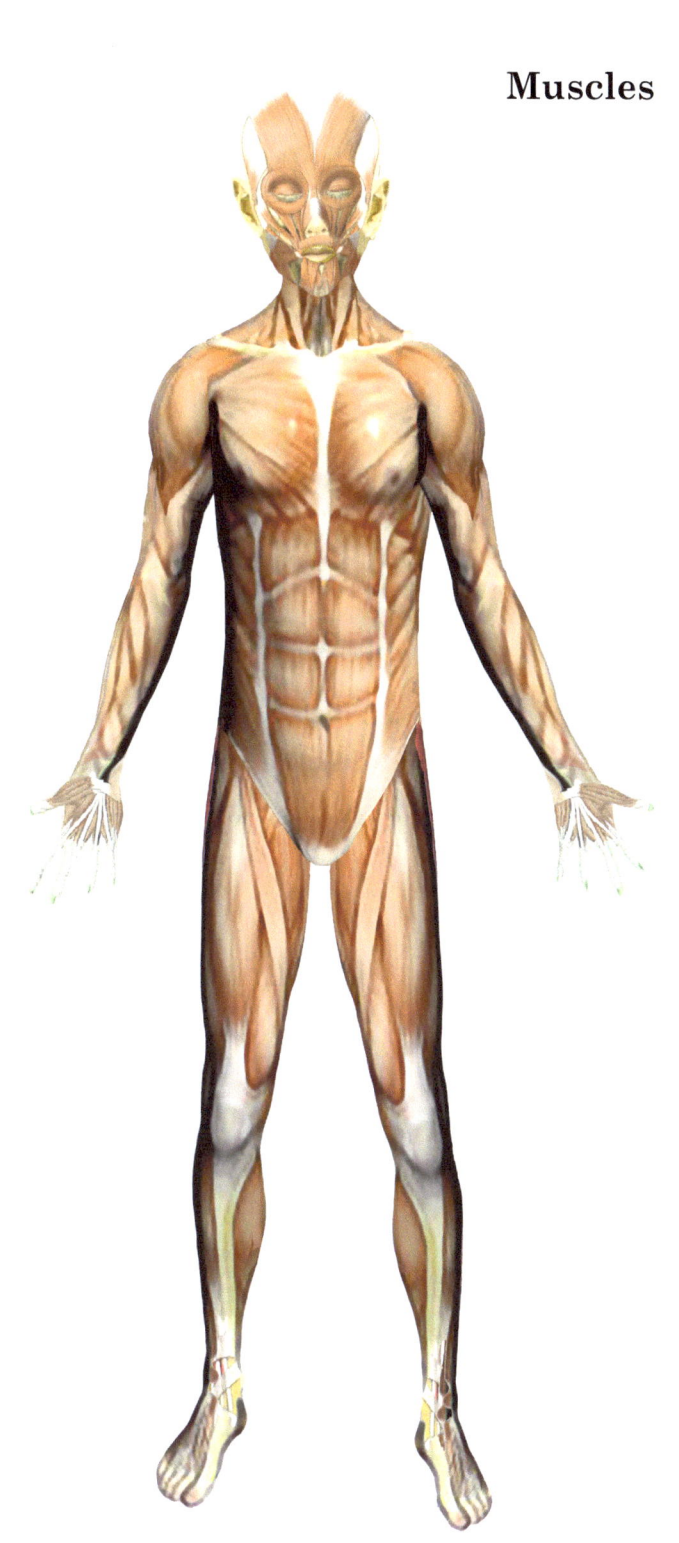

Muscles

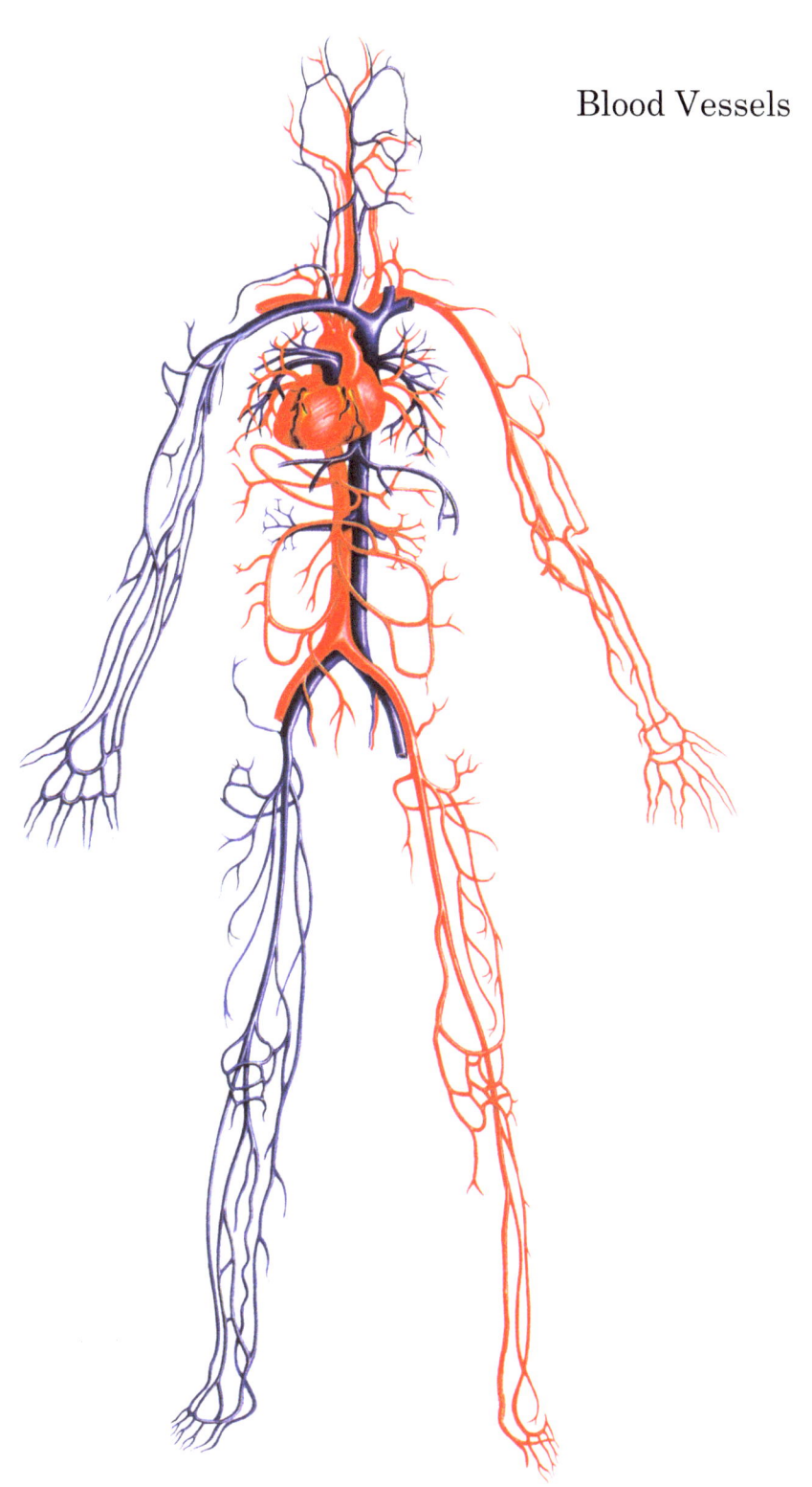
Blood Vessels

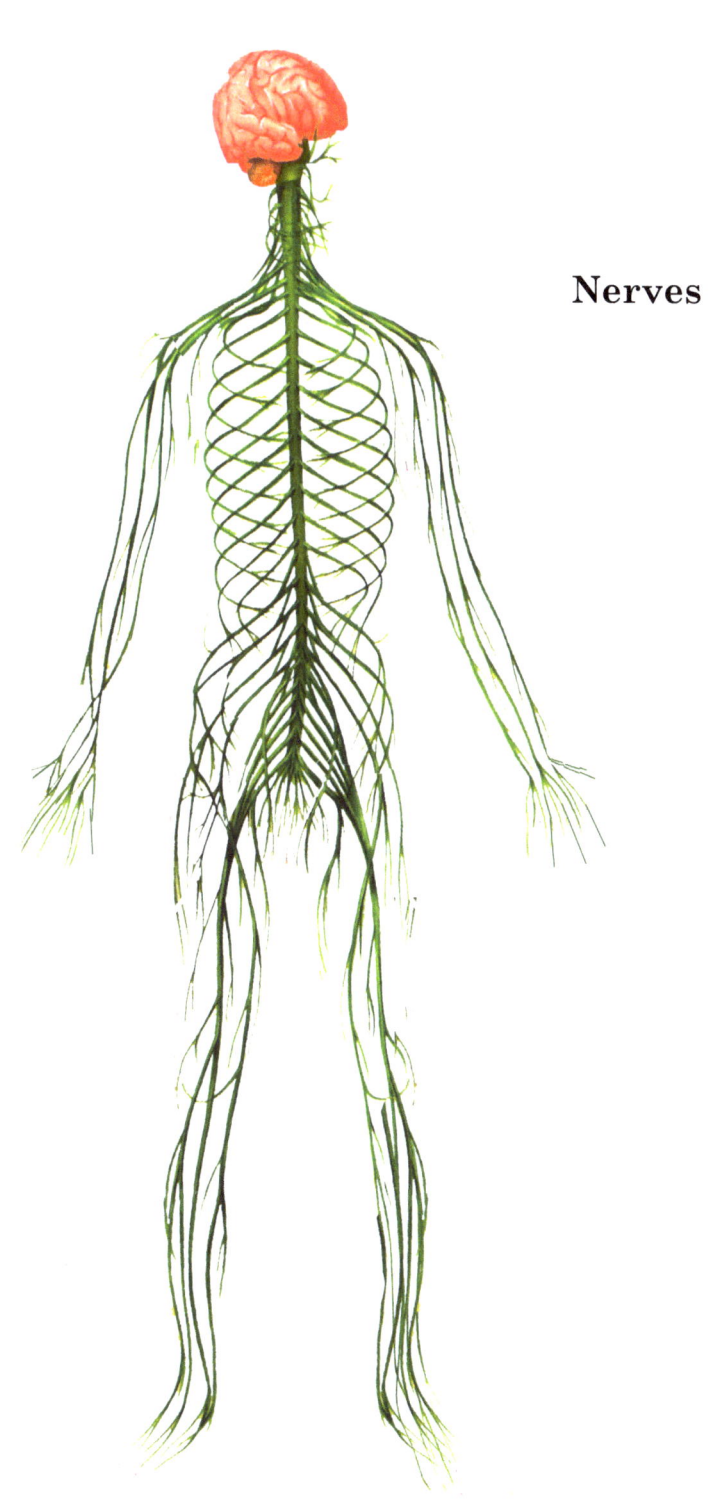

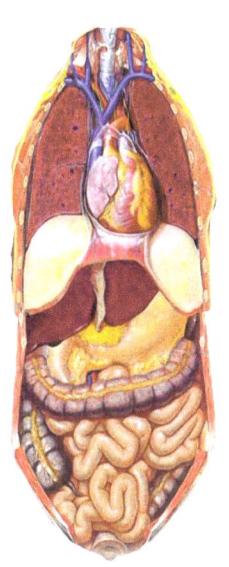

Abdominals

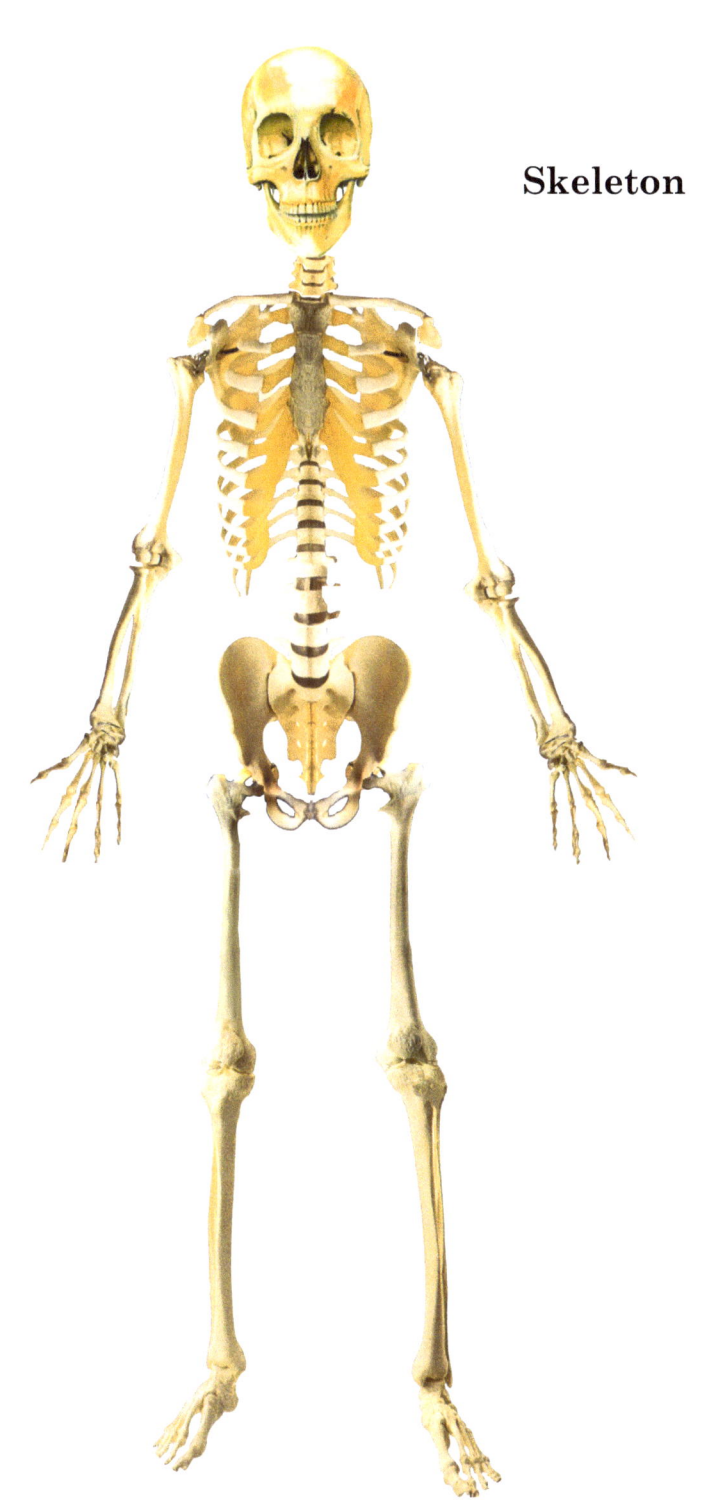

Skeleton

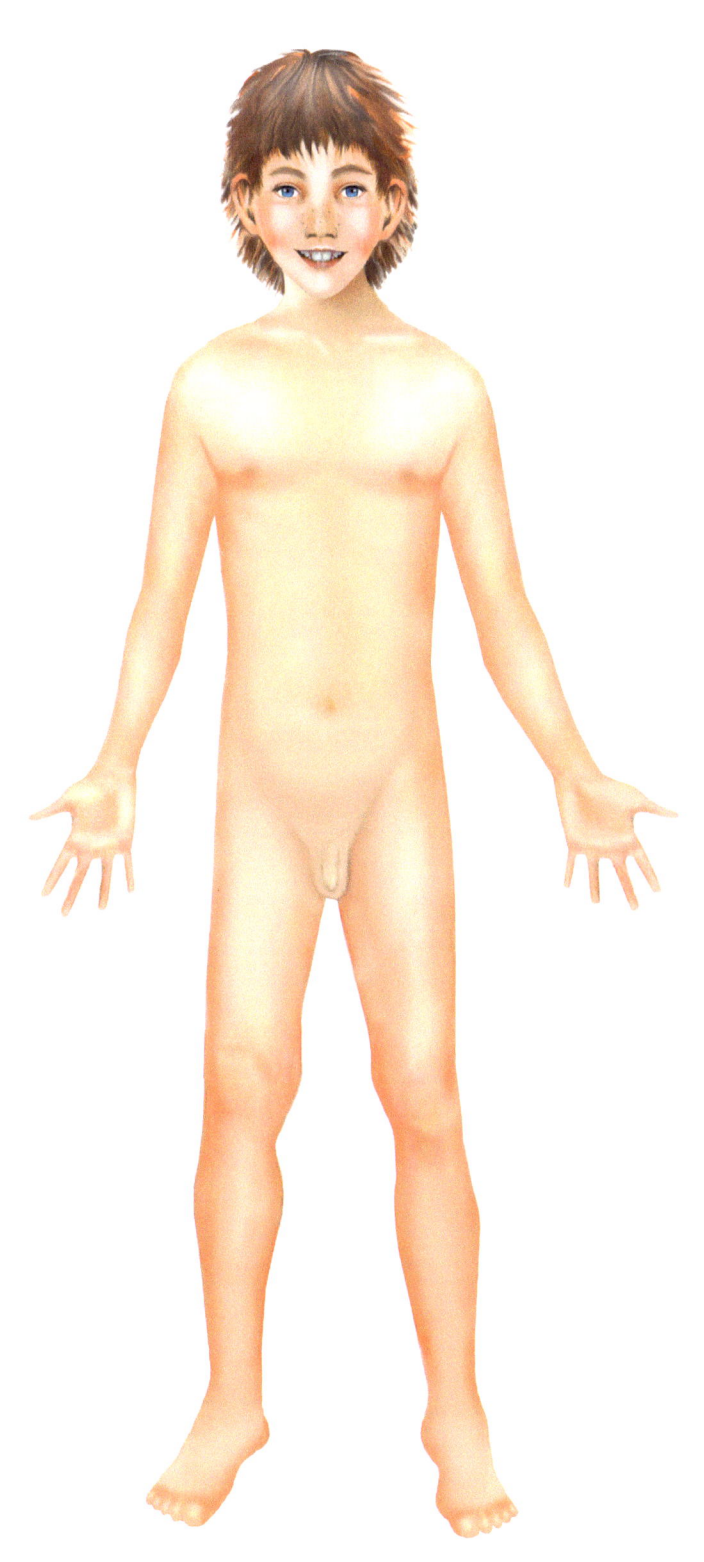

www.ingramcontent.com/pod-product-compliance
Lightning Source LLC
LaVergne TN
LVHW072112070426
835510LV00002B/23